Chasing the Ivy

Also by Maureen Almond

Tailor Tacks	(pub Mudfog 1999)
Oyster Baby	(pub Biscuit 2002)
The Works	(pub Biscuit 2004)
Tongues in Trees	(pub New Writing North 2005)
Recollections	(pub Flambard 2008)

Maureen Almond

Chasing the Ivy

*Love and best wishes Ann —
I hope you enjoy this*

*Maureen x.
14/11/09.*

Biscuit Publishing

First published 2009 by
Biscuit Publishing Ltd.,
PO Box 123, Washington
NE37 2YW
Great Britain
www.biscuitpublishing.com

ISBN 978 1 903914 37 3

Cover picture (Ivy) © 2009 by Maureen Almond
www.maureenalmond.com

Typeset by Mike Wilson, Bridlington

This book is dedicated to
my precious daughter Marie and to dear James
in celebration of their wedding on 12 September 2009

Acknowledgements

I owe a great debt to Professor Stephen Harrison, of Corpus Christi College, Oxford, who has continued not only as my scholarly adviser, but has given me his unstinting support and encouragement. My thanks too, to Professor David West whose translation and notes I used extensively during the preparation of these poems and for his personal support; also to Dr. Peter McDonald who kindly read the early version of my manuscript and provided encouragement, and to my colleagues and mentors at the University of Newcastle, most especially my personal tutors Professor Sean O'Brien and Professor John Moles. Thanks also go to Professor Jerry Paterson for his guidance and support.

Some of the poems collected here have previously been published in *The Pelican, Iris, Lit, New Writing from the School of English, Newcastle University* (Eds. W.N. Herbert and Sean O'Brien), *Le Journal de BabeLg*, and on the *Tower Poetry* website. In addition poems have been presented at *Ancient Verses, Modern Voices* Conference, University of Durham, *On the Frontier* Classical Association Annual Conference, University of Newcastle (2006), *Augustan Poetry Day*, University of Durham, *The Classical Reception Studies Network Conference*, The Open University, Milton Keynes, *Perceptions of Horace Conference* at University College London during 2007, *Horace Live and Kicking* at the Lit and Phil, Newcastle-upon-Tyne, *The Poetry and Translation Conference* at University of Stirling, July, 2008, *Rendering Horace* for The Departmental Research Seminar of the Department of Classics at Glasgow and the committee of the Classical Association of Scotland Glasgow & West Centre, October, 2008, *The Classical Association Annual Conference* hosted by University of Glasgow, April, 2009 and broadcast on BBC Radio 3 as part of *The Essay: Greek and Latin Voices* series, (2007).

Thanks are also due to many poetry friends who have listened and commented as I have worked through versions of the poems and to Dr. Josephine Balmer, Andy Croft, Dr. Barbara Graziosi, Professor Lorna Hardwick, Dr. Luke Houghton, Dr. Jennifer Ingleheart, Professor John Talbot, and Brian Lister at Biscuit Publishing, for their support and encouragement.

Contents

9 Introduction

13 Ode to Horace *(after Horace Ode 1.32 Poscimus si quid)*
14 Ode to God and Man *(after Horace Ode 1.12 Quem virum aut heroa)*
15 Ode to My First Poetry Tutor *(after Horace Ode 1:17 Velox amoenum)*
16 Ode to An Arvon Course Writer *(after Horace Ode 1.9 Vides ut alta)*
17 Ode to Naive Poets *(after Horace Ode 1:22 Integer vitae)*
18 Ode to a Community Arts Worker *(after Horace Ode 1.13 Cum tu, Lydia)*
19 Ode to 22nd November, 1990 *(after Horace Ode 1.37 Nunc est bibendum)*
20 Ode to Seamus Heaney *(after Horace Ode 1.10 Mercuri, facunde)*
21 Ode to the Poetry Establishment *(after Horace Ode 1.8 Lydia, dic, per omnis)*
22 Ode to the S.S. Poetry *(after Horace Ode 1.14 0 navis, referent)*
23 Ode to the Possible Future Laureate (and his current hot girlfriend) *(after Horace Ode 1.5 Quis multa gracilis)*
24 Ode to the Editor *(after Horace Ode 1.1 Maecenas atavis edite)*
25 Ode to a 'Proper' Poet *(after Horace Ode 1.3 Sic te diva)*
26 Ode to Poets (as a last resort) *(after Horace Ode 1.2 lam satis terris)*
27 Ode to George and Tony *(after Horace Ode 1.6 Scriberis Vario)*
28 Ode to the Poet in His Own Little World *(after Horace Ode 1:26 Musis amicus)*
29 Ode to the North *(after Horace Ode 1.7 Laudabunt alii)*
30 Ode to Fortune *(after Horace Ode1.35 0 diva, gratum)*
32 Ode for a Maker of Performance Poets *(after Horace Ode 1.15 Pastor cum traheret)*
33 Ode to the Mate of a Wandering Poet *(after Horace Ode 1.36 Et ture et fidibus)*
34 Ode to the Poet Deserting His Roots *(after Horace Ode 1:29 Icci, beatis)*
35 Ode to New Voices *(after Horace Ode 1.4 Solvitur acris hiems)*
36 Ode to the Poetry Professor at the End of Term *(after Horace Ode 1:27 Natis in usum)*
37 Ode to Young Poets *(after Horace Ode 1:21 Dianam tenerae)*
38 Ode to Michael i. m. Michael Donaghy *(after Horace Ode 1:24 Quis desiderio)*
39 Ode to Death *(after Horace Ode 1:28 Te maris et terrae)*
41 Ode to the Non-Poet Partner *(after Horace Ode 1.11 Tu ne quaesieris)*
42 Ode to Demon Writers *(after Horace Ode 1:18 Nullam, Vare, sacra)*
43 Ode to an Offended Fellow Poet *(after Horace Ode 1.16 0 matre pulchra)*
45 Ode to the Net-worker *(after Horace Ode 1:23 Vitas inuleo)*

46 Ode to a Love-Sick Fellow Poet *(after Horace Ode 1.33 Albi, ne doleas)*
47 Ode for Myself *(after Horace Ode 1:19 Mater saeva cupidinum)*
48 Ode to the Wrinkly Writer *(after Horace Ode 1:25 Parcius iunctas)*
49 Ode to the Student Returning *(after Horace Ode 1.30 0 Venus, regina)*
50 Ode to Ambition *(after Horace Ode 1.31 Quid dedicatum)*
51 Ode to an Agnostic Poet *(after Horace Ode 1.34 Parcus deorum cultor)*
52 Ode to a Simple Poet *(after Horace Ode 1.38 Persicos odi)*
53 Ode to Stephen *(after Horace Ode 1:20 Vile potabis)*

The Women Poems

54 Anon
55 Cinera's Message to Venus
56 Leuconoe's Ultimatum
57 Lydia
58 Myrtale
59 Pyrrha
60 Reluctant to Love (Chloe)
61 Talk of Love (Lalage)
62 The Devil in Me (Glycera)
63 With Love to Horace from Canidia
64 Tyndaris Accepts Horace's Nightcap

Introduction

My aim with this collection is to set up a detailed and complex world of poetic patronage and relationships as a parallel for Horace's interactions with his patron, Maecenas, and other literary figures in Augustan Rome. As in *The Works* (pub. Biscuit, 2004), I have taken the poems away from the originals in terms of form and style, and recontextualised them to give them a truly contemporary feel. Although I am not a Latin speaker I do glance at the Latin and try to glean extra nuance from it in terms of interpretation and additional colour. My version of *Odes*, Book I is reset into the world of contemporary poetry as I know it; a world of writing, reading, reflection, public readings, personal successes and failures, tutoring, residencies, Arts Council grants (patronage), admiration and jealousies, acceptance and rejection.

In *Odes*, Book I Horace examines his position against other poets. When he writes about war, he chooses a lower and 'non-war' genre as in *Odes* 1.6. He can accommodate war, as in *Odes* 1.37, but I suspect, like myself, that Horace felt impotent, unable to affect what happened in the wider world around him. Certainly impotence, both sexual and in a more general sense, is another recurring Horatian theme. He used irony as a means of expression and release. Referring to the work of Marina Tsvetaeva in *Poetry Review[1]* Elaine Feinstein says she used 'irony as a way of keeping deep feeling at a distance': maybe Horace did too and I certainly do!

Self-doubt is also clearly a theme, though Horace's confidence develops over Books 1-3. In 1.1 he asks for classic status; by 3.30, he is demanding his own coronation as a poet. I try to lay more emphasis on amusingly constructed self-deprecation than real self-doubt. Horace was certainly negotiating his way up the poetic ladder, and making his (successful) bid for star status. In the last line of 1.1 (which I take with some irony), he says, 'My soaring head will touch the stars.'

Especially when he professes poetic greatness, Horace pokes fun at himself, which I believe shows more confidence than he would have us believe. Socially, he has made it as a protégé of Maecenas (as in 1.1), and his insecurity is really about finding his place in the hall of fame.

The Greek lyric poets are significant in book 1, especially Alcaeus (1.32), as is the clash with love-elegy (e.g. 1.33). Horace uses it as a further means of defining himself. He writes about love, but in a less romantic and more ironic way. My take on love has always been somewhat ironic (see my previous collection, *Oyster Baby* (pub. Biscuit,

[1] 'Close To The Bone', *Poetry Review*, Volume 96:2, Summer, 2006 [p.57]

2002)). I well remember, after reading from *Oyster Baby* at the Voice Box, Royal Festival Hall, London, in February, 2003, a gentleman saying, "You're a bit of a fraud; behind your somewhat dark poems, the love still comes through." I was delighted.

Age is important too: when the Odes came out, Horace was 42, mature and middle-aged in Roman terms. He was more relaxed (and less angry) than in his earlier poetry. More mellow, though not without social and poetic ambition. I like to see myself as more mellow than angry; as for poetic ambition; it's very definitely there. I don't want to sit quietly in the corner of a darkened room and write just for myself. I want people to engage with my writing and, like Horace, I'd like to think it will live on after me: now I really am being ironic!

Apart from anything contained within the work, there are biographical parallels between myself and Horace. At the time of writing this collection, I too am mature in years (the exact level of maturity is for me only to know!) and we are both ironic in outlook, negotiating a position in a complex literary scene. Horace began not as professional poet but in public service (he was a court clerk). I worked as an administrator and personnel manager in the Probation Service for over twenty years.

I see myself as a down-to-earth, gritty female from Teesside, so there are some telling differences too which will, I hope, add edge and interest. Individual Maecenas figures don't exist any more and it is much tougher to carve a path in this literary world as it is today, but as ever I am grateful for the support and encouragement I continue to receive both from New Writing North and from Arts Council North East, who are, in many senses, my patrons.

Keeping, just for a moment, on the theme of 'grit,' I have included a section of 'women poems.' Horace is dismissive of the women in his poems and I felt it was time we heard from them, so here, I give them voice – allow them, based on the Odes in which they appear, to answer him back (accepting of course, that these women probably never existed at all!)

This collection is my attempt at an ironic account of a poet making her ironic way through the bunkers and sand traps of the current literary scene.

'Moreover, with a nice taste and care in weaving words together, you will express yourself most happily, if a skilful setting makes a familiar word new.'

Horace
Ars Poetica (46-48)

'In ground open to you all you will win private rights, if you do not linger along the easy and open pathway, if you do not seek to render word for word, as a slavish translator.'

Horace
Ars Poetica (131-134)

'Good poets blend their experience of literature and their experience of life in a hugely complex operation which they themselves do not fully understand.'

David West
Horace Odes I: Carpe Diem (83)

Ode to Horace

(after Horace Ode 1.32 Poscimus si quid)

If ever I've toyed with you before,
I pray, as I curl up with you in my still bed,
and play with words to outlive me,
come and drop your flaccid thoughts
into my ears to make them flap,
my Roman poet

first turned on for me by a man of Latin
who, whether battling with students
or relaxing by the oar-sprayed Isis,
still emails on Archilochus and Virgil,
on Ovid and Alcaeus,
on you, with your lyrical spirit
your lyrical tongue.

I glorify you, Horace, my bed-time book,
welcome at mind-feasts;
poet who's lit up my efforts:
Give me your worldly insights
whenever I think of you.

Ode to God and Man

(after Horace Ode 1.12 Quem virum aut heroa)

Is everything I am a gift from God
and should I sing his praises for my lot?
Or maybe thanks are due to Mr. Davies
my Titan teacher for the scholarship?

Perhaps it's down to you, great-granda Bernard,
that fiddling echoes round inside my head;
and songs play out through you, great-grandma Bridget,
from Donaghmoyne to Durham to the Tees.

This hybrid, small-p poet-politician
who swerves from forked-tongue talking when she can
should probably thank Patrick and the Green Fool
whose words were brought across from Monaghan.

Poteen helped make our Hamill-poesy sweeter.
No matter how it happened I thank God
that mother's fire combined with father's lyrics
has meant ancestral music can live on.

Ode to My First Poetry Tutor

(after Horace Ode 1:17 Velox amoenum)

Denise, you gave up England's northern coast
to go down under where the surfers play.
Your Grove Hill voice has moved in as my muse –
her mithering fills the block at Clockhouse Wood.

Beyond these iron gates there's no false coupling.
Our verse will trickle, free; it won't be damned.
Our wet-behind-the-ears-kid poems will ripple
the sluggish surface of that speechless Tees.

Remember how you nudged my writer's arm?
I'm glad to say it goes from strength to strength.
So come back home and share in my contentment.
Come on, Denise; we've suffered for our art.

Be molly-coddled in my wood, it's safe.
I'll keep the poet dog-eat-dogs at bay.
Complete your script and toast your oeuvre with Asti:
We'll not make cock-brained, piss-heads welcome here,

or ratbag critics to crush your confidence
with bad reviews. You've no need to be scared
of back-biters who'd sink their poison in –
there's no one here to dress you down to size.

Ode to An Arvon Course Writer
(after Horace Ode 1.9 Vides ut alta)

Mist creeps up on Lumb Bank like a sly old fox
and the valley shivers.
Death-curled leaves clack against branches brittle as bone,
to settle on the narrow, lonely path.

Bring in the logs, fill the scuttle
my precious young writer,
drop your money into the honesty box;
draw whites from the kitchen
and reds from the dining room rack.

During this special week,
forget everything you've left behind.
Don't worry about the poems whirling in your head
or the ones left floating over editors' desks.
Your work will settle in its own good time.

Stop thinking about tomorrow and its needs,
live for today. You have no ties, look around,
enjoy yourself while you're young.

Now's the time to pour the wine
and leave the experience of my grey hair, my little protégé.
Look at all the bright young things around you;
find a new life with them.

It was good while it lasted,
but now, join our young tutor over there,
the one who's been giving you the eye,
and fly.

Ode to Naïve Poets

(after Horace Ode 1:22 Integer vitae)

We genuine poets don't have to take the flack
that other writers take from jealous peers.
We're never crushed by critic profiteers
who just can't wait to stab us in the back

and even when we stray beyond our limits
into topics never visited before,
our talent is described as *fresh and raw*
we're not dismissed as *just a bunch of dim-wits.*

In fact when I express myself from Teesside
and leave my comfort zone to head down south,
the famous fear what might come out my mouth:
they grit their teeth while swallowing their pride.

And yet that Hughes' wild dog creeps in and howls.
With ears pricked and razor teeth he blocks
my mind and keeps it blank before he locks
ideas down to consonants and vowels.

Put me with those certain, sexy women,
your Shapcotts and your Duffys and your Olds.
Though what I have to say won't be as bold
I'll use the little gift that I've been given,

to crack this nut and make my writing ring.
I want to get my feet under the table:
dear tutor, tease my words then I'll be able
to love my poems at last and make them sing.

Ode to a Community Arts Worker
(after Horace Ode 1.13 Cum tu, Lydia)

Robbie, what's she got that I don't have,
this latest little protégée of yours?
The way you keep on bigging up her poetry
makes me sick.

And if I have to hear you one more time
say, *bet we haven't heard the last of her*
I promise you I'll scream because believe me,
I'm fed up to the back-teeth.

Quite literally my own words start to choke me
watching hers impress you. It seems a flash
of pen or a well-thrown line and that's you sunk.
She'll eat you for breakfast.

Why do you never listen to me, you pillock.
The bitch is using you to suit her ends.
What makes you think she'll want the likes of you
when once she's made it?

Whereas you and me, Robbie, we've grown together.
We've scratched each other's backs, you get my drift!
We should try to get to know each other better.
Nothing dodgy though!

Ode to 22nd November, 1990

(after Horace Ode 1.37 Nunc est bibendum)

At last we breathe a huge sigh of relief.
Now let's sit back and watch the fun and games.
Time to stock committee rooms with claret:
till lately just one glass was out of reach,

the birch-keen crazy woman saw to that.
Power-mad, she tanked-up on the Falklands
then with her rotten cronies took our capital,
and poll-taxed poor pensioners and poets.

Now she's brought to heel: (though having once
survived like Cleopatra and her ships),
rejected by her own, a sober thought,
she sees the proper battle on her hands.

While in the wings the hawkish Michael waits
to peck this honourable monster carcass clean.
But the Carlton Club's most honorary member
stares her crushed society in the face.

She chose her poison, took it like a man
enjoyed defeat and didn't do a U-turn.
The media didn't march the Iron Lady
before us as a rusty washed-up has-been.

Ode to Seamus Heaney

(after Horace Ode 1.10 Mercuri, facunde)

Seamus, spiritual descendant of Patrick,
the Green Fool who showed us in fireside rhythms
and the glowing embers of his cindered words
the starkness of his land;

I write of you, king of all living poets,
music-maker of everything that happens,
for you are the mischievous assuager
of our stolen lives.

When you were young, some people ranted on
about how you moved south, taking their histories,
wanting whatever you said, to be *nothing.*
You taught the tick tick

of a constable's bike; *arithmetic and fear.*
Now you're my guide, tempting me out of my shell
with forlorn ideas of success and fame.
You teach me my place.

Having gathered up my insubstantial words,
in your own golden hand, you write; *a woman
dabbles in verses and finds they are her life.*
Keep fiddling, you say.

Ode to the Poetry Establishment

(after Horace Ode 1.8 Lydia, dic, per omnis)

For God's sake you lot have you never heard
of killing someone softly with your love!
That Ricky-Rhymer hangs on every word
since being told he's guided from above.

And now he won't set foot inside our schools,
won't dip his toe in residential waters;
They're just a bunch of comprehensive fools
he says of would-be rhyming sons and daughters.

He used to roll his sleeves up with the rest
but now he's fat on complimentary grapes.
You've made him soft by telling him he's blest
and dropping all those goodies on his plate.

What happens if he's bruised by bad reviews?
What if, poor lad, he's beaten in the chase?
You coddle him and keep him in the news;
it's your fault if he falls flat on his face.

It's down to you if he can't take the heat,
you made him feel ethereal and unreal.
You never let him stand on his own feet.
It's you he'll see as his Achilles heel.

Ode to the S.S. Poetry
(after Horace Ode 1.14 O navis, referent)

You call yourself a Flagship! a literary liner
for such as me to cruise away their days.
Don't make me laugh, you're listing on new waves.
You make me sick.

Your passengers have stripped you bare. It seems
a re-fit's what you need, and while you're here
best drop the erotic colours from your flagpole;
they've led you astray!

Crippled by a cargo of translation
that drags you down below the water line
you creak and whine and make your invocation,
to the god Obscure.

Iced quatrains and measured Canberra couplets
help me ride the storm, but even so
concrete fore and aft is not enough
I'm tossed like a cork,

and bounced about by sexy stanza makers
with ropey rhymes that skim along your decks.
Unrated prats like me with no commission –
We keep you afloat.

Plot a middle course between the rocks
of old volcanic form and swirling spume.
I'm sick to death of sailing round in circles.
Cut me some slack.

Ode to the Possible Future Laureate

(and his current hot girlfriend)
(after Horace Ode 1.5 Quis multa gracilis)

Who is she making up to now,
that long-haired redhead,
that blarney-kissed girl,
that temptress in the red dress?
And in a jealous rage,
will he too,
end up firing her big, hard lines,
        along with her mascara?

She's such a smooth talker;
great at pouring oil on troubled water,
and he just can't see through it.
He really believes this golden-tongued girl
        is all his;
that she'll always be there, at his beck and call –
naïve fool!
Is he blind or what?
Can't he see what's brewing – God help him?
She's never going to give him her rhythms for nothing,
or donate her verse and stilettos to Oxfam!

As for me,
I'm done with her sort once and for all.
I've given up life in the fast column,
hung up my epics with my motor-bike clips
and slipped into something more comfortable:
suitable sonnets to drop gently
in the Poetry Society's lap.

Ode to the Editor

(after Horace Ode 1.1 Maecenas atavis edite)

By now my work and you are quite good friends;
You canon-maker, sweetheart, darling Ed!
Some people use their voice to bill and coo,
or make hot sounds to stick inside your head.

Some lofty academics make their names
by spreading out their great iambic feet.
They catch you up in wild syllabic storms;
they put their plumped-up verse beyond your reach.

Some gravitate towards you at a gig
to drop their latest project in your ear.
They say they simply want to test the water
but meanwhile, *would you like another beer?*

Some dangle their awards before your eyes:
you're hypnotized by Gregories on chests,
and when they say they're willing to perform
stark naked in your slush-pool, you accept!

So still the wild exotic sucks you in
with word gymnastics, double pun and worse.
With sexy mouths some put you on a promise
increased sales for publishing their verse.

My *mind* is all *I* open by the way.
You need to know that *my* words aren't just verbals.
And as for me I'm not prepared to lie
to earn my laurels.

Ode to a 'Proper' Poet

(after Horace Ode 1.3 Sic te diva)

God help her now she's joined *our* little ship.
She'll need her charms to help her ride the storm;
best flash her eyes and pout her poetry lip.

This favoured girl, dear friends, is yours and mine.
With sycophantic words she earns her laurels.
She wants the stars: let's hope they help her shine.

She fights sestina storms and haiku hell,
but when she finds she's dashed against a rock-
hard editor, her sonnets twist and swell.

She'd rather turn her back on simple rhyme.
For her the breath is king, and yet she scans
pedantically till each foot toes the line.

The girl's got form. She stresses everywhere.
Hot property, she rushes in with lies.
Creative thought comes naturally to her.

So like us all she flies too near the sun.
One day her fuck-me words will melt like wax.
She'll plummet to the depths, her free flight done.

Or else her lusty need for recognition
will see the monstrous oeuvre she's conceived
entangled in a maze of definition.

And all of us keep adding to the mess,
so many poets thrusting at the stars.
Wars are made of less.

Ode to Poets (as a last resort)
(after Horace Ode 1.2 Iam satis terris)

Thundering boots have echoed round us twice
and once a man, by stretching out his arm,
stirred such an angry storm the whole world shook.

A fragile, stuttering king coughed over rubble
while fear took root and countries changed their shapes.
Though Vestas kept fires burning hearths were lost.

More recently a bolt out of the blue,
made ivory towers collapse. The city fell.
Our sixty years of nearly-calm was past.

We talk of valour, right and friendly fire
supposedly to make us feel less dead.
Our texted, unsaid love-words float on dust.

What sort of God can let us fight like this?
A tender god could quickly spike our heels
with love and turn us all away from war.

Who else is there to trust except our poets?
And if there's use in art, what better use
than civilizers writing protest verse?

Ode to George and Tony

(after Horace Ode 1.6 Scriberis Vario)

If only *we* had Owen or Sassoon:
such fighting poets keep an eagle eye.
They'd see two nations going it alone
and knock our bare-faced courage into line.

Tony, I'll never claim to understand
nor try to write in praise of your success.
Our views ignored, we soldier up with George;
put mass destruction theories to the test.

But me, I'm just a mediocre poet,
I scratch out words on scraps of information.
I leave important issues to the 'biggies'
and marvel at the topics put in motion.

Were *I* to try and honour you, with say
a sonnet, well it wouldn't help a bit.
My baby-rhymes would likely undermine
your triumphs, and I'd make you look unfit.

The daily grind of husbands, wives and poets,
I'll peck around at those, that's more my class.
Then sometimes when I'm out and on the razzle
I'll ditch the dead and raise a victory glass.

Ode to the Poet in His Own Little World

(after Horace Ode 1:26 Musis amicus)

I've thrown my worries in the River Tees
and I'm off to join the fairies yet again.
I couldn't give a damn which Imam rules
the oil supply nor what financial whiz-kids

cocooned inside the City's one square mile
drone on about; forget them. But I ask
that those who see things through a writer's eye
praise poets like Katrina, Jackie, Cynthia.

These women are my source of inspiration.
Without such feisty poets I'd be lost.
They plummet hidden depths to pluck out words
and make them burn forever in our souls.

Ode to the North
(after Horace Ode 1.7 Laudabunt alii)

Let others bull up poncey southern culture
or pussy-foot about on P.Soc. ground.
Ignore them when they brag about their capital
with slimy little words; they earn their crowns.

So what, big deal. I've mouthed off at the *Voice Box*.
I've surfed the latest academic waves.
I've chewed the fat at A-list poetry places
but give me dead-end bars where *Jesus Saves*.

And all you strictly top-drawer magaziners
who sing Arts Council tunes with rounded vowels,
best cock an ear for northern-sounding voices
we've no plans yet for throwing in the towel.

Get yourselves up north where Tyne and Wear
and Tees, all overflow with gritty words.
Don't tie yourself in knots with sweet-tongued small-talk,
impress *New Writing North* with simple verse.

Look my friends, I'm offering a gift-horse.
Don't look it in the mouth, lift up your hearts
and come with me behind my northern shield
to help me fire our straighter literary darts.

Let's build a prize-land we can call our own.
I'll take the risk if you will. Let's make hay.
Go get yourself a lager – better still
Newcastle Brown to help you seize the day.

Ode to Fortune

(after Horace Ode1.35 O diva, gratum)

Chance guides everything in Ironopolis.
Round here, we say, *that's life; it's just a fluke.*
You make it or you end up on the scrap heap.
All we ever ask's an even break.

Old ironmen just want a fighting chance,
and so do those who're not of steely stock.
All of us who live here by the Tees
pray we'll have another stroke of luck.

We all got on our bikes in nineteen fifty
and pedalled way beyond our cast-iron world.
We left the north in droves; the intelligentsia
and the workers and the bosses. Everyone

needs Fortune, even poets. That's the reason
they huddle close together in a scrum
of seething academic literati
in case scholastic posts should tumble down.

And always here, the mother of invention
with hand-me-downs, and let's make-do-and-mends.
Her *never-mind, we'll make the best of it*;
her *let's-forget-it* shrugs black-lead her eyes.

Fortune's left the North-East coast, it seems,
but loyal to old ways, we still have hope,
(if only in small pockets). We hang on,
we stand and watch while chance flies out the door.

The good-time-girls and entrepreneurial chancers,
the short-term do-good-Johnnies, all have gone:
Even friends who shared each other's burdens
have disappeared now the trough's run dry.

God bless our Teesside poets and politicians
who stick their necks out trying to spread a word
of optimistic caution about the north.
Let's hope along the line, they shake things up.

And shame on us up here who dump our own,
then join the trendy set of dog-eat-dog.
We rifle what we can and leave the scars;
forget what makes us great and run away.

Our young fear nothing now, not consequence
nor fate nor God, so, Fortune, please come back
from oily eastern shores. Re-hone us all.
Re-fabricate your workers and your bards.

Ode for a Maker of Performance Poets

(after Horace Ode 1.15 Pastor cum traheret)

When a DJ drags me off into the floodlights
(a traitor to his own poetic cause),
and drops me, his *class act* onto the deck
to grope around the half-lit stage in fear

I admit I'm flattered; wouldn't you be?
Then I hear the mutterings from the floor,
how *her sort are the thin edge of the wedge*;
how *she'll kill this place and ruin Davey's cred.*

A boy-band on before me gets applause
that brings the house down; I begin to shake.
Too late to run and hide, I've burnt my bridges,
I sense I'm going to end up on my arse.

Now the DJ, silly bugger's terrified;
despite the cheapo beer he's organised
it's dawned on him he's serving neither cause:
by playing away we'd had it from the start.

He's well and truly caught, pathetic dope,
between the usual rock and poetry's hard place.
Too scared to sing my praises he lopes off
to find himself a safer watering hole.

I shouldn't have submitted to this coupling;
and the masters of the web have barely started.
Miles from poetry and everything it means
they'll U-tube me and stick me up on Face-Book.

Ode to the Mate of a Wandering Poet

(after Horace Ode 1.36 Et ture et fidibus)

This round's on me, come on, lads, name your poison
and pass the ciggies round. Who wants pork scratchings?
Let's all enjoy ourselves. I've sweated blood –
to get this little shindig off the ground.

As soon as Dave comes in we'll give three cheers.
Thank God he's back on the northern scene again.
He'll read some poems and have high-fives especially
for our mate Danny, here, his boyhood hero –

the two of them cut poetry teeth together
in Boro pubs. We've all turned out tonight
so make the most of it. Let's have a slam
and blast our voices way beyond the Tees.

We mustn't let these Geordies or the Mackems
outdrink us Smoggies on a night like this.
Scatter poetry pamphlets on the benches
and pile our hard-back words up on the table,

then feast your eyes on all the Tyne and Wear boys
they'll slap our writing buddy on the back.
Because he packed his poems and played away
they'll cling to him like ivy, just you watch.

Ode to the Poet Deserting His Roots
(after Horace Ode 1:29 Icci, beatis)

So, old mate, you want to make your name.
To see yourself as one of the elite?
You think you'll conquer Hooray Henry hearts
by buffing up your scruffy state-school vowels?

You've no chance pal. Your glottal-stops will slip.
No poet-scholars will ever big you up
when scripts by them are hijacked and killed off.
They'll tease you but they'll keep you in your place.

Academic poetry boys still rule OK!
They flex their lyric muscles on the canon.
You think they want to hear what's in *your* mouth
even though you watch your p's and q's?

Now you cross your t's and dot your i's
you think you've cracked it do you – think you're in?
Well better think again you silly sucker,
you'll find your novelty will soon wear thin

and we won't want you either once you trim
your verse like them, on Sunday afternoons.
When you escape your accent then the Tees
will trickle up towards the Cleveland Hills.

Ode to New Voices
(after Horace Ode 1.4 Solvitur acris hiems)

Now the cool beat's ended, things are heating up.
All sorts of wordsmiths crawl from the paperwork
to graze upon erotica. Their lines are galvanised.
They stir us with hot text, they burn our eyes.

The time's come for the rest of us to gel our hair,
Lynx up, and sacrifice our fawning wishes.
What's more, dreamers among us can reveal,
we no longer diss those chasing two-book deals.

But then, what does it matter in the end?
Death kicks the writer's door as hard as any.
We're not Falernian. We won't be savoured.
And our few poor words? They'll be remaindered.

Let us remember, as we make our pitch:
Not one of us will have the final say.
Come on! Which pricked-up youth, laid in his bed,
which girl, will dwell on anything we've said?

Ode to the Poetry Professor at the End of Term
(after Horace Ode 1:27 Natis in usum)

All right, don't let the beer go to your heads –
just enjoy a drink but keep the noise down.
Good poets would hold their booze better than this,
you're not some engineering air-heads on the lash.

I've come in here to have a quiet pint
not bandy beered-up words with all of you.
Show your class and lose the traffic cone
and if you want me here at chucking out,

then stop this fighting talk. You, Abby's brother,
why don't you fill us in about your love life.
No ale for me unless you dish the dirt;
don't be shy, your secret's safe with me!

Whoever she is she's got her claws in you,
best not to fight it, lad, that's my advice.
Once they've got you wrapped around their finger
you might as well give in, there's no escape.

Ode to Young Poets
(after Horace Ode 1:21 Dianam tenerae)

Girls, don't be scared to fantasise, sex sells,
you boys as well, erotica is hot.
Use basic instinct: that's what hits the spot.

Young women watch Madonna light the stage.
She revels in her form, gets in your head
to stir things up that otherwise were dead.

Lads, why not take the pop stars as your models?
Their stubbled sex appeal is ripe for books.
Arouse with rhyme what Robbie does with looks.

Those two could break your block, stuff empty words
with promise, give your editors a ball
and drive the weakling-writers to the wall.

Ode to Michael

i.m. Michael Donaghy
(after Horace Ode 1:24 Quis desiderio)

There's competition for elegy
and why not for this much loved poet,
called to sing by the Muse of Tragedy
too long before his time? But then that's fate.
Not even Michael's creative wit,
his warmth and care for fellow poets
could conjure a way out of this one.
All who knew him grieve and weep: he lit
our rooms. You, Simon, aim to recall light:
with your *Patent* and try to make
everlasting bulbs; dull the sun.
But light can't fill a Jupiter shape.
Might Michael illuminate death for our sake
if we work into the night?

Ode to Death

(after Horace Ode 1:28 Te maris et terrae)

Your metre was meticulous, dear Horace;
as fine as sand, and yet you trickle through
the minds of just a sprinkling of scholars.
What did verse gain you?

With brilliance you read the universe,
showed how we are, but yet your tongue is stilled.
And Ovid's too, despite his god-like skill
and metamorphic hands.

Poor Sappho died before her thirst for verse
was quenched, so she's in bits. Lucilius' fresh
eleven hundred unconnected lines
are distant trails.

The words of Alcaeus used to crash and bang
like thunder and lightning in the public ear.
He penned ten Hellenistic scrolls; so what?
they're sound bites now.

In my own time dear Brendan, man of rain,
whose heart stopped once and yet came back to beat
the shadowlands of life and death – he too
will die one day.

One writer's lost in conflict; while another
drowns in slush piles. Others briefly shine
before they burn. Our poets too will dim.
Death catches all,

including me! When breath fades and my flesh
is eaten up by worms, then I'll be speechless.
So grant me shelf-space, please, since there are many
ways of dying.

You up-and-coming writers, thrown around
on crashing poetry waves, best play it safe.
Prosper and grow famous in the hands
that guard the canon.

But don't forget that by ignoring me
you're robbing those who might admire my words.
Be fair, or I may haunt you when I turn
my final page.

I know how busy literary folk can be
but how long would it take you, honestly,
to read me one more time before I'm laid
gently in the archive.

Ode to the Non-Poet Partner

(after Horace Ode 1.11 Tu ne quaesieris)

Just don't ask about it, love. God
decided death should surprise us.
Let's not bother reading the stars.
They'll tell us – nothing.

Look at our border conifers
see how they reduce tidal waves –
angry words to a slight rustle,
and keep on growing.

Those mighty trees are home to birds
on both sides of the fence. The wind
gives them their rhythm, puts things back
on nodding terms.

Think how those trees, despite bent limbs
seize each day and reach for the sky.
Break out the cans, we'll live today.
Tomorrow never comes.

Ode to Demon Writers
(after Horace Ode 1:18 Nullam, Vare, sacra)

Danny, mate, enjoy your amber nectar,
a special pint of brown at friendly fringes.
The tipple of the gods, a one-off binge
is fine because creative life is hard
and even harder still if stone-cold sober!

Who ever saw a canny two-pints writer
get lover's block or cry into his beer?
A drop of good stuff helps unlock ideas.
Know when to stop but don't be lost for words.
Drop your fighting talk, don't diss your peers.

Up here we're all supposed to hold our ale:
Just bear in mind our northern pride's at stake.
Don't make that Gazza no-holds-barred mistake
of gloves-off free-for-alls that end in tears.
Incestuous worlds like ours will see you fail.

First you blow your trumpet then your mind
especially when you've liquor down your neck.
You bandy stanzas, you're a total wreck,
and as for bringing poets down to size –
Talk about the country of the blind!

You'd better keep a tight tongue in your head.
Don't view things through the bottom of a glass.
I've shared a toast or two myself and gassed
with great and good; with famous and unknown.
Let others praise your work: don't praise your own.

Ode to an Offended Fellow Poet
(after Horace Ode 1.16 O matre pulchra)

Ignore my email, trash my sarky poem.
Don't forward junk, it just makes matters worse.
My God, but you're your father's son all right.
Shred the bloody thing!

No women's writing groups, no gender mags
cause laddish authors' droop: they still perform.
No one-too-many, washed-up poetry coach
bangs on quite this much.

Your anger's grabbed you firmly by the balls.
No heated row or threat of sharp reviews,
no casting you adrift from writing circles
makes you shut your trap.

What's said about your poetry isn't true
despite the buzz. If God's name doesn't calm you
nothing will because you've got yourself
into a write frenzy.

I've warned you lots of times about the critics,
the freaks who make and break us at a stroke,
but *you* can't wait to take things to the line;
fire everything up.

The spicy sauce you drizzle on their plate
is not enough to hide your thinned-out verse.
They'll bring you down and tear you limb from limb
then hang you out to dry.

They'll make you eat your words: And this idea,
this view you hold, that most things go my way,
for me the sun will literally reverse,
it drives you red with rage.

Your work is strong, but fury grinds you down.
You plumb the depths and turn your students off.
You need to warm your words or see your class
razed to the ground.

I'll dump the worst of verse (that's yours, not mine!).
Recycle poems, take back all I've said.
We must be friends again: bad blood got me
when I was your age too!

Ode to the Net-worker

(after Horace Ode 1:23 Vitas inuleo)

I see that you're avoiding me again,
as if our friendship posed some sort of threat
(or is it that you know I'm useless to you?)
Whatever, mate, don't panic that *my* work

has topped the slush pile earlier than yours.
Just because somebody's script is rustling
on editors' desks, or brilliant gift-packed poems
are quickening, you're ruffled head to toe!

Trust me Jo, I wouldn't put the boot in,
wouldn't steal your lines or cast a shadow
of doubt on your good words – no need to network.
Your verse is ready; it can hold its own.

Ode to a Love-Sick Fellow Poet

(after Horace Ode 1.33 Albi, ne doleas)

Forget it, Phil, just ditch the fiery redhead.
Stop writing endless poems to *dear sweet Ann.*
Her sort are all the same: they let you down,
her new bloke's not good-looking, but he's strong.

I tell you, lad, all this, it's just a game.
You must remember Ricky, how he worshipped
Bella's form and how he hung on every word.
But Dave was in her sonnets and her bed.

Remember how we said *it'll end in tears,
Bella's going to get what's coming, that's for sure.*
We knew back then how love hurts and how Venus
throws most unlikely pairs into the sack.

And surely you remember *my* fiasco
how I chose a so-called hero who was strong
enough to give me space and let me breathe,
yet decided night and day and tied my tongue.

Ode for Myself

(after Horace Ode 1:19 Mater saeva cupidinum)

Of late, I seem driven by Cupid.
Feelings that had died have struck like lightning,
unexpectedly, again,

ignited, perhaps, by a nightly tipple,
and the idea of having rubbed shoulders
with the T.S. Eliot list.

Such notions set me on a slippery slope.
There's not a hope that Carol Ann or Sheenagh
would see anything in me.

And yet I find I have to toy with them;
swirl them around for flavour as you do
a delicious mouthful of red.

Desire has taken over: when at last
my sturdy pen *is* ready to perform,
idle thoughts are curdling the ink.

Folk keep telling me to act my age. OK!
I'll sacrifice my wilder plans, but please
give me a poet to embrace.

Ode to the Wrinkly Writer

(after Horace Ode 1:25 Parcius iunctas)

The rampant literati seem less keen
to finger scripts or rouse you with their praise.
You used to spread your lines across the page:
now they're locked and frigid.

Young scribes were once among your greatest fans:
these days they never email for your verse
and while you romp round daily with your muse
they write you off.

Soon your skin will wither, and your words
will wrinkle on some Oxfam bargain rack
remaindered by indifference. Mates step back:
your groupies leave you cold.

By looking for acclaim your hopes and dreams
will drive you like the rest of us insane.
Frustration bouncing round inside your brain,
you'll feel neglected: you'll moan

about the happy wannabees who follow
new hot shoots of fame, but what's your quarrel?
You'll have had your time, and so your laurels
grow brittle in tomorrow's frost.

Ode to the Student Returning

(after Horace Ode 1.30 O Venus, regina)

Venus, Muse of lovers everywhere,
why not dump the eloquent well-served south?
Join me here by the Tees' untutored mouth.
This wrinkly writer needs your lyric care.

Bring Eros with his band and Youth: I've heard
that with their help I'd capture hearts and minds;
seduce the academics on the Tyne,
till they embraced me, every thought and word.

Ode to Ambition

(after Horace Ode 1.31 Quid dedicatum)

So what should poets ask of academia
once erudite façades have all been built?
What honours do they seek, what aspiration
ferments their thought until new words pour out?

Not the flowery praise of scholar-poets;
not fruits of southern fame meant as a lure
to so-called fertile ground where poetry houses
are slowly starved of funding, that's for sure!

Let those with sponsors labour on their epics,
let them trim verse back not let it roll.
Let them toast their dry nouveau-success
gained from emptying hearts and baring souls.

I've no desire to ride their trendy wagon,
go celestial, have strange places for my head.
I'd rather have a cocoa then rest easy
in my loosely-sprung, uncontroversial bed.

So let me keep my common-grounded lyrics,
my colloquial tone, my gritty northern voice.
Let me prize these gifts in ripe old age.
Simple talent; good reason to rejoice.

Ode to an Agnostic Poet

(after Horace Ode 1.34 Parcus deorum cultor)

I do still pray, but like a little kid
I only shut one eye to think of God:
The other eye's possessed by poetry
and glaring at my mates who're obsessed too.

Being Catholic, mea culpa, I retrace
my steps across familiar ground, although
you'd get a coach and horses through the hole
in faith that until now has served me well.

The creative course I've taken makes me reel
then shakes me to the core. I'm being drowned
by the tidal wave of knowledge in my head.
Yes, I've gained an insane wisdom, but I'm lost

and the instability's led me straight to hell
where I'm dizzied in a labyrinth of learning,
by the twists and turns of too much information.
It's more than I can bear without God's help.

For only God has power to ring the changes
ensure the first is last and last is first.
With one shrill cry, sweet chance can snatch the ivy
from the laureate's head and crown the little man.

Ode to a Simple Poet
(after Horace Ode 1.38 Persicos odi)

What's with all this fancy talk m'dear?
Stuff your silver words they leave me cold.
I don't need measured lines, well-formed and folded,
or accents buffed until they all but shine.

For goodness sake stop fussing over lyrics;
admittedly exotic lyrics suit you
and me as well, but still I think we two
should make sweet music, have ourselves a break.

Ode to Stephen

(after Horace Ode 1:20 Vile potabis)

Don't just pore over my meagre emailed words,
come up and get ratted on my hard lines
knocked back with Newcastle Brown
in proper bottles I bought from Yarm offy
especially for you Stephen,
distinguished, kindly scholar,

while you're applauded by ranks of students
            on the banks of the Isis;
and lecture theatres, shaken by your knowledge,
echo your professorship.

You can savour vintage Latin poems
and enjoy classics from the Italian grape,
but no Sicilian vines, Roman hills or conjugations
will flatten my Northern beer
or soften my rough voice.

Anon

(based on Horace Ode 1.14, O navis, referent)

I'm having an affair (though of the heart);
Windswept yes, but not at all at sea.
Truth be known, we're better off apart.
Ships passing in the night, that's you and me.

I've trimmed my sails; I'm heading out to sea:
back on course with little thanks to you.
We passed some time together, let it be.
Get over it, that's what I plan to do.

Mine's a brand new course. I'd say it's you
who's gone adrift and made me stronger.
Get over it, that's what I plan to do
I won't be kept at anchor any longer.

Surely you must see you've made me stronger
truth be known, we're better when apart.
I won't be kept at anchor any longer
I'm having an affair, though of the heart.

Cinera's Message to Venus

(based on Horace Odes 4:1, Intermissa, Venus)

Dear girl, come up and see me any time.
Your reputation's safe: I'm still on fire.
Ignore the snowy roof, look in the grate.
In any case I wanted to enquire

about your trip and how things went with Horace.
I hope he's fit and well and full of beans.
He reckoned once to love me, did you know?
(I doubt he even knows what true love means).

Looking back I really don't recall
his lust for me was ever sweet as such.
I know he never moved the earth for me.
Some things I forget, but not that much!

Is it true he's searching round for his libido?
Has he asked you if you'd like to give a hand?
Good luck old girl, you're surely going to need it,
he'd problems carrying out your hard command.

I wish him all the best, don't get me wrong
but obviously I have more staying power.
So as I say, just pop in when you want.
I'll buy the wine. Don't bother bringing flowers.

Just one more thing, you'll find me wearing purple.
It's not a sign of mourning or of age.
It's such a sexy colour don't you think,
for girls who just can't wait to turn the page?

Leuconoe's Ultimatum

(based on Horace Ode 1.11, Tu ne quaesieris)

Again you throw that old familiar line,
saying we should live but for the day.
I fall for it and let you have your way:
I shelve my plans and tell you that it's fine.

You play it cool, and joke, *who needs a ring?*
No promises are made, perhaps you think
there's no need for commitment as I sink
my head down on your chest and bite my tongue.

But listen up, my dear, my softer side
is dying. You're the one who'll end up worn
by lust that ebbs and flows just like the tide.
Seize the night, my love, you've earned my scorn.
This time, like you, I'm here for the ride.
White waiting days will vanish with the dawn.

Lydia

(based on Horace Odes 1:8, Lydia, dic, per omnis,
1:13, Cum tu, Lydia, and
1:25, Parcius iunctas)

From the start, you had your eye on me.
Like some sort of rabid voyeur
you looked on while I nibbled necks
and others bruised my white shoulders.

My horseplay made your stomach churn
yet you imagined stroking my hips.
Jealousy burned you up; you pretended
yours were the teeth marks on my lips.

As for my making men soft,
soft they were not – nor womanlike!
I never put a man off his stroke
or stopped one throwing beyond his mark.

You were wrong, I've not aged, I've matured.
I'm rounded, fuller-bodied with a fruity whiff.
I've a good nose. You'd like to seize the day,
wouldn't you; take a little sip?

This playgirl, her face lifted regularly
by the eternal youth she clings onto
is no old rag. She's up to her eyes in toyboys.
They bang her door, ring her bell, form a queue.

Myrtale

(based on Horace Ode 1:33 Albi, ne doleas)

If I had loved you would I have felt shackled?
Would I have cursed Venus' sense of humour?
Did you ever think I might just have settled
for the best I could get at the time?

And later, when we were alone in the dark
did you realise I had other offers on the table?
Yes I was wild; perhaps I even had the mark
of madness. Maybe that's why I tried to cling on.

Had you done the same, you'd not be alone now.
You make me laugh, the way you give advice.
Why on earth should anyone listen to how
you, a confirmed bachelor, managed your life?

I, on the other hand, have found myself a lover.
When I wrap around him he knows he's been
chained; but get this, honey, he loves it!
Turns out I wasn't forever green.

Pyrrha

(based on Horace Ode 1:5 Quis multa gracilis)

Acting on advice my mother gave,
my aim in life's to be an old man's darling:
I've no desire to be a young man's slave.

So when I get it on, stop all your snarling
because the time I spend with those young bucks
is nothing more than practice, mere harling

for experience that doesn't come from books.
Don't waste your pity those lads know the score.
I'm hooked in by their lifelines not their looks.

So ponder this: it's you I'm coming for.

Reluctant to Love

(Chloe)
(based on Horace Ode 1:23 Vitas inuleo)

You insist that it's time to be bolder,
saying, *little green shoot, please don't weep.*
I feel myself squirm and my skin starts to creep,
as you settle your hand round my shoulder.

Then you tell me, *stop running to mother*
you should leave young-girl habits behind.
I wonder, what is it you have on your mind,
what you mean by forsaking all others.

I hate how you can't seem to look in my eyes,
how you focus instead on my breasts.
I object to the way that you try to impress
with your numerous sweet lyric-lies.

Whatever you're hoping to gain by your charms
I'm just not disposed to fall into your arms.

Talk of Love
(Lalage)
(based on Horace Ode 1:22 Integer vitae)

You hear me sweetly laughing; sweetly speaking,
my name is carried to you on the breeze.
Inside the deep dark woods you sing my praises.
Your own voice echoes back between the trees:

you celebrate your purity of heart.
Your love is in the clouds and there it hovers;
you practice gentle kisses on your arm
and hope to finally seal our fate as lovers.

And then it starts; the bragging to your mate:
You ramble on and boast how you'll protect me.
You tell him that unarmed you scared a wolf.
I hear you now. I've got you to a t.

You'd swim the widest rivers for my sake
and march across the desert thirty days.
You'd leave your home and trundle in the sun.
You love me in a thousand different ways.

(And I'm supposed to be the chatterer!)
I know, I know, you'll shout it from the houses.
I take it back, you're not a sheep dressed up.
Forgive me love; you're not all mouth and trousers

The Devil in Me
(Glycera)
*(based on Horace Ode 1:19 Mater saeva cupidinum, and
Horace Ode 1.30 O Venus, regina)*

Cut your pathetic chat-up line.
I'm not your sweet thing
and well you know it!
This glow that sets you alight
is nothing to do with love –
everything to do with instinct –
       mine!

I'm hot; who needs your heart
or Cupid cards, or flowers?
Who needs your fine fancy words?
You don't have to put me on a pedestal,
or sacrifice your lads' nights.
I'm no more interested in the long term
      than you are, pet.

Rambling on about love – get a grip:
you're such a wimp.
Look into my eyes, for goodness' sake;
Don't you recognise a 'come-on'
      when you see it?

With Love to Horace from Canidia

(based on Horace Epode 3, Parentis olim,
Horace, Epode 5, At, o deorum, and
Horace, Epode 17, Iam iam efficaces)

Go on, admit it, Goths, they turn you on,
and I'm the wicked bitch who got you hooked;
bewitched you with my scary green-gelled spikes,
my street-wise ways; my secret night-life looks.

I'm the hag who used black-lacquered nails
and raised the man-blood in your boyhood veins.
Remember when the time came to unzip me,
you got entangled in my jacket chains?

Then there was that grassy afternoon, when
unable to resist my snow-white skin,
you traced the tattooed feathers on my shoulder
and twirled my silver nose ring with a grin

'til I promised you an afternoon a week
for your fetishes. You treat me like a whore.
I curse your love life. May you have no wife
or children then you'll come to me for more.

Tyndaris Accepts Horace's Nightcap
(based on Horace Ode 1:17, Velox amoenum)

This face, darling, could bring wise men to war,
it doesn't need your macho-man protection.
I'm used to being the centre of attention,
it's jealousy I seek, not country air.

The smell of goat's best sampled from afar,
as for lyre-skills, dear, that's pure invention,
a ruse, to make you think it's my intention
to sooth your muse, not follow my own star.

I'll gladly join you in a glass of red,
but I'm not for interweaving through the night.
By ten I'm usually ready for my bed,
to dream of Cyrus' passions at their height.

And turning men to pigs: that's in your head.
You do it to yourselves – put out the light.

Notes

Ode to God and Man (p.14)
Hamill is the family name of the author.
Poteen is an Irish alcohol made from potatoes.
The Green Fool is a novel by Irish Poet Patrick Kavanagh, who was, as is the author's family, from County Monaghan.

Ode to An Arvon Course Writer (p.16)
Lumb Bank at Heptonstall, Hebden Bridge, West Yorkshire, was the home of Ted Hughes and Sylvia Plath and is now a writing centre owned and run by the Arvon Foundation.

Ode to Naïve Poets (p.17)
The *'certain, sexy women'* referred to here are the acclaimed contemporary poets Jo Shapcott, Carol Ann Duffy and Sharon Olds.

Ode to Seamus Heaney (p.20)
The Green Fool is an autobiographical novel by the Irish Poet P. J. Kavanagh.

Ode to the S.S. Poetry (p.22)
Canberra here refers to the cruise liner which was said to have concrete fore to keep it level in the water.

Ode to the Editor (p.24)
The Eric Gregory Award is open only to people up to the age of 30.

Ode to the Poet in His Own Little World (p.28)
The poem refers to SJ Litherland and Cynthia Fuller, Wearside poets, and Katrina Porteous, from Northumberland. All three are gritty, determined yet gentle women poets who work vigorously at their art.

Ode to the North (p.29)
P.Soc is a popular shortened way of referring to The Poetry Society.
The Voice Box is a reading venue in the Festival Hall, London.
Lumb Bank (see earlier note in respect of 'Ode to An Arvon Course Writer'
Sylvia Plath is buried in Heptonstall Cemetery not far from the Lumb Bank Centre.
New Writing North is based on Tyneside and supports the work of artists and writers.

Ode to the Mate of a Wandering Poet (p.33)
Middlesbrough in Teeside is known locally as The Boro.
Geordies is a colloquial term for people from Tyneside and *Mackems* is a colloquial term for those who live in Sunderland. *Smoggies* is a colloquial name for those from Teesside.

Ode to Michael i. m. Michael Donaghy (p.38)
Michael Donaghy was an accomplished musician as well as a poet.
Simon Armitage's poem, 'Patent,' is in memory of Michael Donaghy.
One of Michael Donaghy's collections is called *'Conjure.'*

Ode to Death (p.39)
Brendan is the Irish poet Brendan Kennelly, who, following quadruple bypass surgery, wrote a collection called *The Man Made of Rain* which tells of the shadowlands between life and death.

Ode for Myself (p.47)
The T S Eliot Prize shortlist for 2005 was Polly Clark, Carol Ann Duffy, Helen Farish, David Harsent, Sinead Morrissey, Alice Oswald, Pascale Petiit, Sheenagh Pugh, John Stammers and Gerard Woodward.

The Women Poems (p.54-p.64)

The author acknowledges the scholarly argument that these women may never have existed as individuals, but has chosen, nevertheless, to give the characters a voice.

Anon
Cinera's Message to Venus
Leuconoe's Ultimatum
Lydia
Myrtale
Pyrrha
Reluctant to Love (Chloe)
Talk of Love (Lalage)
The Devil in Me (Glycera)
With Love to Horace from Canidia
Tyndaris Accepts Horace's Nightcap